THE YEAR'S AT THE SPRING

AN ANTHOLOGY OF BEST-LOVED POEMS
ILLUSTRATED BY HARRY CLARKE

GILL&
MACMILLAN

Gill & Macmillan
Hume Avenue, Park West, Dublin 12
with associated companies throughout the world

www.gillmacmillanbooks.ie

ISBN 9780717158225

This book was created and produced by Teapot Press Ltd

Introduction and biographies by Fiona Biggs
Edited by Fiona Biggs and Elisabeth Golding
Designed by Tony Potter

Printed in PRC

This book is typeset in Garamond and AT Sackers Classic Roman.

5 4 3 2 1

THE YEAR'S AT
THE SPRING

CONTENTS

*'And the dead robed in red and sea-lilies
overhead sway when the long winds blow.'*
Drawing by Harry Clarke to illustrate
The Dying Patriot by James Elroy Flecker, a
poem included in the original edition of
The Year's At The Spring.

INTRODUCTION

In his introduction to the original edition of this book, published in London in 1920, the poet Harold Monro says that 'the best poetry is always about the earth itself and all the strange and lovely things that compose and inhabit it. . . . The first object of poetry is to give pleasure. Pleasure is various, but it cannot exist where the emotions or the imagination have not been powerfully stirred.'

The poems in this volume are not just about the simple pleasure of happiness, although we certainly find reminders of times when we were happy, and cheerful verses for

children, too. The poetry here also affords us the pleasure of recognising that we are not alone, that others have experienced similar failings, disappointments and lost opportunities, and have succumbed to the all-too-human tendency to be fascinated by that which disturbs us. When this anthology was first published, it must have seemed that we were on the brink of a bright new era. The cloying sentimentality of the Victorians was a thing of the past, and the 'war to end all wars' had finally come to an end, with as yet no foreshadowing of the even greater conflict that would afflict the world within fewer than 20 years. A new age had dawned, with all its possibilities of new discoveries and limitless opportunities, and *The Year's at the Spring* burst forth as an expression of and reflection on the hope within all of us that makes living possible. With very few exceptions, all the poets included in the anthology were contemporary. According to Monro, 'all except eight of its authors are living and writing'. Two notable exceptions were the much-loved Robert

Browning and John Keats. Thomas Hardy, while writing contemporaneously, was of another age, and could probably be categorised as 'an eminent Victorian', although his work eschewed the sentimentality of that era. Many of the poets included were not big names at the time of publication, nor, indeed, did they go on to achieve lasting fame. They were chosen not for their fame, but for how their poetry fit the aim of the collection, which was, unequivocally, 'to give pleasure'. An example of a poem that is entirely successful in this is Margaret Mackenzie's lyrical 'To the Coming Spring', which vividly conveys that sense of delighted anticipation that affects us all after a long winter as we find the first small signs of spring, everything 'we had forgotten in the Winter's gloom'.

Some of the poems in the original volume have been replaced in this edition, being somewhat out of step with modern tastes and sensibilities. The 'War' poets have been retained, although Monro believed, not without reason, that most of the war verse produced during the First World War was 'definitely and unmistakably bad' and that 'as the years pass, fewer "War poems" can still be read with pleasure, the incidents which gave rise to them having become dim in human memory'. He did, however, concede that those selected for the anthology had literary merit. Probably included at the time as a nod to the prevailing sense of anger and grief at the loss of so many young lives, a century later the sense of futility, waste and shattered dreams seems to have increased rather than diminished with the passage of time. Also included in this edition are several works by the poets of the 1916 Rising – they tell of love, beauty, God and the grandeur of nature; yet another reminder of cruelly wasted youth, potential and talent. The original anthology was 'adapated to the tastes of almost any age, from ten to ninety, and may be read aloud by grandchild to grandparent as suitably as by grandparent to grandchild'. Some additional children's poems have been included here, including William Allingham's eminently recitable but unexpectedly sinister 'The Fairies'. Irish poets were notable by their absence, with W. B. Yeats, Patrick Chalmers and James Stephens representing the entire national *oeuvre*. The balance has been redressed by the inclusion of works by James Joyce, Francis Ledwidge, Oscar Wilde, William Allingham, Pádraig Pearse, Thomas MacDonagh and Joseph Mary Plunkett.

When the book was published, *The Bookman* told its readers that 'The subjects . . . provide an admirable field for the genius of Harry Clarke.' Following their success with *Tales of Mystery and Imagination* by Edgar Allan Poe, illustrated by Irish artist Harry Clarke, Harrap had commissioned Clarke to produce 12 black and white and 12 colour full-page plates for *The Year's at the Spring*, as well as 22 decorative black and white drawings. He varied his style depending on the subject matter of the poems: here we have the full range, from his trademark silhouettes to his exquisite watercolours.

The extraordinary watercolour accompanying Rupert Brooke's 'The Dead' depicts a noble-visaged 'Honour, come back as a king, to earth', his throne embedded in the faces of the young dead of the Great War. Clarke brings a curious mix of freedom and wistfulness to the simple black and white illustration for Patrick Chalmers's 'If I had a Broomstick', and he captures exactly a child's fantasy world in the elaborate portrayal of mermaids for Queenie Scott-Hopper's 'Very Nearly!' The images sometimes recall his macabre Poe illustrations, but the reader will be taken with the melting, flowing spirits of Lettice D'Oyly Walters's 'All is Spirit and Part of Me' and the delightful ring of dancing fairies of Rose Fyleman's 'Alms in Autumn'. For the most part, the colour palette is pale and subtle, although the plate for E. J. Brady's 'A Ballad of the Captains' is stronger in tone, while G.K. Chesterton's 'Donkey' is an awkward, dun beast in a dull landscape (the pedestrian thumbnail sketches ranged alongside this poem show none of Clarke's hallmark genius). As always with Clarke, the black and white plates are more detailed, with the swashbuckling fleet in 'A Ballad of the Captains' reigning triumphant. Dipping in to this anthology of thoughtful poems and exquisite illustrations will hopefully, almost a century on, give pleasure once again, and put Harry Clarke centre stage for an Irish audience.

April

APRIL, April,
Laugh thy girlish laughter;
Then, the moment after,
Weep thy girlish tears!
April, that mine ears
Like a lover greetest,
If I tell thee, sweetest,
All my hopes and fears,
April, April,
Laugh thy golden laughter,
But, the moment after,
Weep thy golden tears!

William Watson

The Fiddler Of Dooney

WHEN I play on my fiddle in Dooney.
　　Folk dance like a wave of the sea;
My cousin is priest in Kilvarnet,
My brother in Mocharabuiee.
I passed my brother and cousin:
They read in their books of prayer;
I read in my book of songs
I bought at the Sligo fair.
When we come at the end of time
To Peter sitting in state,
He will smile on the three old spirits,
But call me first through the gate;
For the good are always the merry,
Save by an evil chance,
And the merry love the fiddle,
And the merry love to dance:
And when the folk there spy me,
They will all come up to me,
With 'Here is the fiddler of Dooney!'
And dance like a wave of the sea.

William Butler Yeats

16

The Lake Isle of Innisfree

I WILL arise and go now, and go to Innisfree,
And a small cabin build there, of clay and wattles
made:
Nine bean-rows will I have there, a hive for the
honeybee,
And live alone in the bee-loud glade.
And I shall have some peace there, for peace comes
dropping slow,
Dropping from the veils of the morning to where the
cricket sings;
There midnight's all a glimmer, and noon a purple glow,
And evening full of the linnet's wings.
I will arise and go now, for always night and day
I hear lake water lapping with low sounds by the shore;
While I stand on the roadway, or on the pavements
grey,
I hear it in the deep heart's core.

William Butler Yeats

Cradle Song

FROM groves of spice,
O'er fields of rice,
Athwart the lotus-stream,
I bring for you,
Aglint with dew
A little lovely dream.

Sweet, shut your eyes,
The wild fire-flies
Dance through the fairy neem;
From the poppy-bole
For you I stole
A little lovely dream.

Dear eyes, good-night,
In golden light
The stars around you gleam;
On you I press
With soft caress
A little lovely dream.

Sarojini Naidu

The Donkey

WHEN fishes flew and forests walked
    And figs grew upon thorn,
Some moment when the moon was blood,
Then surely I was born;
With monstrous head and sickening cry
And ears like errant wings,
The devil's walking parody
On all four-footed things.

The tattered outlaw of the earth,
Of ancient crooked will;
Starve, scourge, deride me: I am dumb,
I keep my secret still.

Fools! For I also had my hour;
One far fierce hour and sweet:
There was a shout about my ears,
And palms before my feet.

Gilbert Keith Chesterton

A Memory

YOU remember, dear, together
   Two children, you and I,
Sat once in the autumn weather,
Watching the autumn sky.

There was some one round us straying
The whole of the long day through,
Who seemed to say, 'I am playing
At hide and seek with you.'

And one thing after another
Was whispered out of the air,
How God was a big, kind brother
Whose home is in everywhere.

His light like a smile comes glancing
Through the cool, cool winds as they pass,
From the flowers in heaven dancing
To the stars that shine in the grass.

From the clouds in deep blue wreathing
And most from the mountains tall,
But God like a wind goes breathing
A dream of Himself in all.

The heart of the Wise was beating
Sweet, sweet, in our hearts that day:
And many a thought came fleeting
And fancies solemn and gay.

We were grave in our way divining
How childhood was taking wings,
And the wonder world was shining
With vast eternal things.

The solemn twilight fluttered
Like the plumes of seraphim,
And we felt what things were uttered
In the sunset voice of Him.

We lingered long, for dearer
Than home were the mountain places
Where God from the stars dropt nearer
Our pale, dreamy faces.

Our very hearts from beating
We stilled in awed delight,
For spirit and children were meeting
In the purple, ample night.

George William Russell

After a Year

AFTER a year of love
Death of love in a day;
And I who ever strove
To hold love in sure life
Now let it pass away
With no grief and no strife.

Pass – but it holds me yet;
Love, it would seem, may die;
But we cannot forget
And can not be the same,
As lowly or as high,
As once, before this came.

Never as in old days
Can I again stoop low;
Never, now fallen, raise
Spirit and heart above
To where once life did show
The lone soul of my love.

None would the service ask
That she from love requires,
Making it not a task
But a high sacrament
Of all love's dear desires
And all life's grave intent.

And if she asked it not? –
Should I have loved her then? –
Such love was our one lot
And our true destiny.
Shall I find truth again? –
None could have known but she.

And she? – But it is vain
Her life now to surmise,
Whether of joy or pain,
After this borrowed year.
Memory may bring her sighs,
But will it bring a tear?

What if it brought love back? –
Love? – Ah! love died to-day –
She knew that our hearts lack
One thing that makes love true.
And I would not gainsay,
Told her I also knew.

And there an end of it–
I, who had never brooked
Such word as all unfit
For our sure love, brooked this –
Into her eyes I looked,
Left her without a kiss.

Thomas MacDonagh

Sea Fever

I MUST go down to the seas again, to the lonely sea and the
sky,
And all I ask is a tall ship and a star to steer her by;
And the wheel's kick and the wind's song and the white sail's
shaking,
And a grey mist on the sea's face, and a grey dawn breaking.

I must go down to the seas again, for the call of the running tide
Is a wild call and a clear call that may not be denied;
And all I ask is a windy day with the white clouds flying,
And the flung spray and the blown spume, and the sea-gulls
crying.

I must go down to the seas again, to the vagrant gypsy life,
To the gull's way and the whale's way where the wind's like a
whetted knife;
And all I ask is a merry yarn from a laughing fellow-rover,
And quiet sleep and a sweet dream when the long trick's
over.

John Masefield

Tewkesbury Road

IT is good to be out on the road, and going one knows not
where,
Going through meadow and village, one knows not whither or
why;
Through the grey light drift of the dust, in the keen cool rush of
the air,
Under the flying white clouds, and the broad blue lift of the sky.

And to halt at the chattering brook, in a tall green fern at the brink
Where the harebell grows, and the gorse, and the foxgloves purple
and white;
Where the shifty-eyed delicate deer troop down to the brook to
drink
When the stars are mellow and large at the coming on of the night.

O, to feel the beat of the rain, and the homely smell of the earth,
Is a tune for the blood to jig to, and joy past power of words;
And the blessed green comely meadows are all a-ripple with mirth
At the noise of the lambs at play and the dear wild cry of the birds.

John Masefield

A Ballad of the Captains

WHERE are now the Captains
  Of the narrow ships of old
Who with valiant souls went seeking
For the Fabled Fleece of Gold;
In the clouded Dusk of Ages,
In the Dawn of History,
When the ringing songs of Homer
First re-echoed o'er the Sea?

Oh, the Captains lie a-sleeping
Where great iron hulls are sweeping
Out of Suez in their pride;
And they hear not, and they heed not,
And they know not, and they need not
In their deep graves far and wide.

Where are now the Captains
Who went blindly through the Strait,
With a tribute to Poseidon,
A libation poured to Fate?
They were heroes giant-hearted,

That with Terrors, told and sung,
Like blindfolded lions grappled,
When the World was strange and young.

Oh, those cruel Captains never
Shall sweet lovers more dissever,
On their forays as they roll;
Or the mad Dons curse them vainly,
As their baffled ships, ungainly,
Heel them, jeering, to the Mole.

Where are now the Captains
Of those racing, roaring days,
Who of knowledge and of courage,
Drove the clippers on their ways –
To the furthest ounce of pressure,
To the latest stitch of sail,
'Carried on' before the tempest
Till the waters lapped the rail?

Oh, the merry, manly skippers
Of the traders and the clippers,
They are sleeping East and West,
And the brave blue seas shall hold them,
And the oceans five enfold them
In the havens where they rest.

Where are now the Captains
Of the gallant days agone?
They are biding in their places,
And the Great Deep bears no traces
Of their good ships passed and gone.
They are biding in their places,
Where the light of God's own grace is,
And the Great Deep thunders on.

Yea, with never port to steer for,
And with never storm to fear for,
They are waiting wan and white,
And they hear no more the calling
Of the watches, or the falling
Of the sea rain in the night.

Edwin James Brady

A Wave of the Sea

I AM a wave of the sea
And the foam of the wave
And the wind of the foam
And the wings of the wind.

My soul's in the salt of the sea
In the weight of the wave
In the bubbles of foam
In the ways of the wind.

My gift is the depth of the sea
The strength of the wave
The lightness of foam
The speed of the wind.

Joseph Mary Plunkett

In the Wilderness

GAUNT windy moons bedraggled in the dusk
Have drifted by and withered in their shame,
The once-proud Thunder-Terror, fallen tame,
Noses for truffles with unwhetted tusk;
A sickening scent of civet and of musk
Has clogged the nostrils of the Hound of Fame –
But flickering stars are blown to vivid flame
When leaps your beauty from its blazing husk.

Blossom of burning solitude! High things
Are lit with splendour – Love your glimmering ray
Smites them to glory – below them and away
A little song floats upward on the wings
Of daring, and the thunders of the Day
Clamour to God the messages it brings.

Joseph Mary Plunkett

Muineen Water

I KNOW a small lake that sails the palest shadows,
Trailing their frail keels along its waveless sand;
And when isles of grey turf are sunning in its shallows
The far hill is a blue ghost on that land.

Down there my wild heart is startled by the quiet:
The very stones are spying; each tree is a pry;
The light declares against me and exiled from brightness
I stray from those waters invaded by the sky.

But when the sedges fling their bridge of whispers
On waves no moon has hooked, then surely I find,
As that lake into its own dim presence,
A dark calm sinks into my mind.

Frederick Robert Higgins

Father and Son

ONLY last week, walking the hushed fields
Of our most lovely Meath, now thinned by November,
I came to where the road from Laracor leads
To the Boyne river – that seems more lake than river,
Stretched in uneasy light and stript of reeds.

And walking longside an old weir
Of my people's, where nothing stirs – only the shadowed
Leaden flight of a heron up the lean air –
I went unmanly with grief, knowing how my father,
Happy though captive in years, walked last with me there.

Yes, happy in Meath with me for a day
He walked, taking stock of herds hid in their own breathing;
And naming colts, gusty as wind, once steered by his hand,
Lightnings winked in the eyes that were half shy in greeting
Old friends – the wild blades, when he gallivanted the land.

For that proud, wayward man now my heart breaks –
Breaks for that man whose mind was a secret eyrie,
Whose kind hand was sole signet of his race,
Who curbed me, scorned my green ways, yet increasingly
      loved me
Till Death drew its grey blind down his face.

And yet I am pleased that even my reckless ways
Are living shades of his rich calms and passions –
Witnesses for him and for those faint namesakes
With whom now he is one, under yew branches,
Yes, one in a graven silence no bird breaks.

Frederick Robert Higgins

When You Are Old

WHEN you are old and grey and full of sleep,
And nodding by the fire, take down this book,
And slowly read, and dream of the soft look
Your eyes had once, and of their shadows deep;

How many loved your moments of glad grace,
And loved your beauty with love false or true,
But one man loved the pilgrim Soul in you,
And loved the sorrows of your changing face;

And bending down beside the glowing bars,
Murmur, a little sadly, how Love fled
And paced upon the mountains overhead
And hid his face amid a crowd of stars.

William Butler Yeats

Arabia

FAR are the shades of Arabia,
  Where the Princes ride at noon,
'Mid the verdurous vales and thickets,
Under the ghost of the moon;
And so dark is that vaulted purple
Flowers in the forest rise
And toss into blossom 'gainst the phantom stars
Pale in the noonday skies.

Sweet is the music of Arabia
In my heart, when out of dreams
I still in the thin clear mirk of dawn
Descry her gliding streams;
Hear her strange lutes on the green banks
Ring loud with the grief and delight
Of the dim-silked, dark-haired Musicians
In the brooding silence of night.

They haunt me – her lutes and her forests;
No beauty on earth I see
But shadowed with that dream recalls
Her loveliness to me:
Still eyes look coldly upon me,
Cold voices whisper and say –
'He is crazed with the spell of far Arabia,
They have stolen his wits away.'

Walter de la Mare

Full Moon

ONE night as Dick lay half asleep,
  Into his drowsy eyes
A great still light began to creep
From out the silent skies.
It was lovely moon's, for when
He raised his dreamy head,
Her surge of silver filled the pane
And streamed across his bed.
So, for a while, each gazed at each –
Dick and the solemn moon –
Till, climbing slowly on her way,
She vanished, and was gone.

Walter de la Mare

Nod

SOFTLY along the road of evening,
In a twilight dim with rose,
Wrinkled with age, and drenched with dew
Old Nod, the shepherd, goes.

His drowsy flock streams on before him,
Their fleeces charged with gold,
To where the sun's last beam leans low
On Nod the shepherd's fold.

The hedge is quick and green with briar,
From their sand the conies creep;
And all the birds that fly in heaven
Flock singing home to sleep.

His lambs outnumber a noon's roses,
Yet, when night's shadows fall,
His blind old sheep-dog, Slumber-soon,
Misses not one of all.

His are the quiet steeps of dreamland,
The waters of no-more-pain,
His ram's bell rings 'neath an arch of stars,
'Rest, rest, and rest again.'

Walter de la Mare

The Song of the Mad Prince

WHO said, 'Peacock Pie'?
The old King to the sparrow:
Who said, 'Crops are ripe'?
Rust to the harrow:
Who said, 'Where sleeps she now?
Where rests she now her head,
Bathed in eve's loveliness'?
That's what I said.

Who said, 'Ay, mum's the word'?
Sexton to willow:
Who said, 'Green dusk for dreams,
Moss for a pillow'?
Who said, 'All Time's delight
Hath she for narrow bed;
Life's troubled bubble broken'?
That's what I said.

Walter de la Mare

A Dead Harvest

ALONG the graceless grass of town
They rake the rows of red and brown,
Dead leaves, unlike the rows of hay,
Delicate, neither gold nor grey,
Raked long ago and far away.

A narrow silence in the park;
Between the lights a narrow dark.
One street rolls on the north, and one,
Muffled, upon the south doth run.
Amid the mist the work is done.

A futile crop; for it the fire
Smoulders, and, for a stack, a pyre.
So go the town's lives on the breeze,
Even as the sheddings of the trees;
Bosom nor barn is filled with these.

Alice Meynell

November Blue

O HEAVENLY colour! London town
Has blurred it from her skies;
And hooded in an earthly brown,
Unheaven'd the city lies.
No longer standard – like this hue
Above the broad road flies;
Nor does the narrow street the blue
Wear, slender pennon-wise.

But when the gold and silver lamps
Colour the London dew,
And, misted by the winter damps,
The shops shine bright anew –
Blue comes to earth, it walks the street,
It dyes the wide air through;
A mimic sky about their feet,
The throng go crowned with blue.

Alice Meynell

The Shepherdess

She walks – the lady of my delight –
A shepherdess of sheep.
Her flocks are thoughts. She keeps them white;
She keeps them from the steep;
She feeds them on the fragrant height,
And folds them in for sleep.

She roams maternal hills and bright,
Dark valleys safe and deep.
Into that tender breast at night
The chastest stars may peep.
She walks – the lady of my delight –
A shepherdess of sheep.

She holds her little thoughts in sight,
Though gay they run and leap.
She is so circumspect and right;
She has her soul to keep.
She walks – the lady of my delight –
A shepherdess of sheep.

Alice Meynell

1914 III: The Dead

BLOW out, you bugles, over the rich Dead!
There's none of these so lonely and poor of old,
But, dying, has made us rarer gifts than gold.
These laid the world away; poured out the red
Sweet wine of youth; gave up the years to be
Of work and joy, and that unhoped serene,
That men call age; and those who would have been,
Their sons, they gave, their immortality.

Blow, bugles, blow! They brought us, for our dearth,
Holiness, lacked so long, and Love, and Pain.
Honour has come back, as a king, to earth,
And paid his subjects with a royal wage;
And Nobleness walks in our ways again;
And we have come into our heritage.

Rupert Brooke

The Great Lover

I HAVE been so great a lover: filled in days
So proudly with the splendour of Love's praise,
The pain, the calm, and the astonishment,
Desire illimitable, and still content,
And all dear names men use, to cheat despair,
For the perplexed and viewless streams that bear
Our hearts at random down the dark of life.
Now, ere the unthinking silence on that strife
Steals down, I would cheat drowsy Death so far,
My night shall be remembered for a star
That outshone all the suns of all men's days.
Shall I not crown them with immortal praise
Whom I have loved, who have given me, dared with me
High secrets, and in darkness knelt to see
The inenarrable godhead of delight?
Love is a flame: — we have beaconed the world's night.
A city: — and we have built it, these and I.
An emperor: — we have taught the world to die.
So, for their sakes I loved, ere I go hence,
And the high cause of Love's magnificence,

And to keep loyalties young, I'll write those names
Golden forever, eagles, crying flames,
And set them as a banner, that men may know,
To dare the generations, burn, and blow
Out on the wind of Time, shining and streaming....

These I have loved:
   White plates and cups, clean-gleaming,
Ringed with blue lines; and feathery, fairy dust;
Wet roofs, beneath the lamp-light; the strong crust
Of friendly bread; and many-tasting food;
Rainbows; and the blue bitter smoke of wood;
And radiant raindrops couching in cool flowers;
And flowers themselves, that sway through sunny hours,
Dreaming of moths that drink them under the moon;
Then, the cool kindliness of sheets, that soon
Smooth away trouble; and the rough male kiss
Of blankets; grainy wood; live hair that is
Shining and free; blue-massing clouds; the keen
Unpassioned beauty of a great machine;

The benison of hot water; furs to touch;
The good smell of old clothes; and other such –
The comfortable smell of friendly fingers,
Hair's fragrance, and the musty reek that lingers
About dead leaves and last year's ferns....

                                             Dear names,
And thousand others throng to me! Royal flames;
Sweet water's dimpling laugh from tap or spring;
Holes in the ground; and voices that do sing:
Voices in laughter, too; and body's pain,
Soon turned to peace; and the deep-panting train;
Firm sands; the little dulling edge of foam
That browns and dwindles as the wave goes home;
And washen stones, gay for an hour; the cold
Graveness of iron; moist black earthen mould;
Sleep; and high places; footprints in the dew;
And oaks; and brown horse-chestnuts, glossy-new;
And new-peeled sticks; and shining pools on grass; –
All these have been my loves. And these shall pass,
Whatever passes not, in the great hour,
Nor all my passion, all my prayers, have power

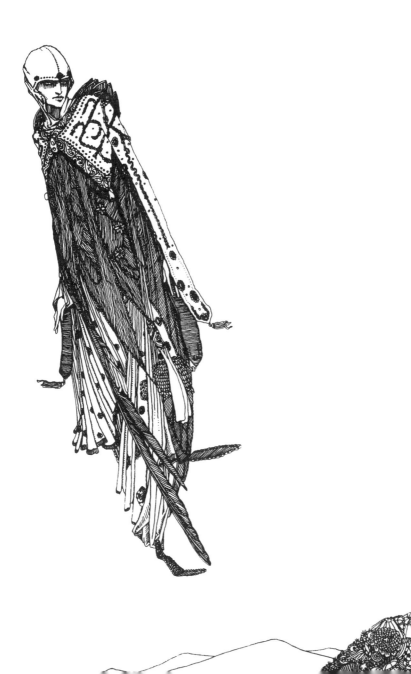

To hold them with me through the gate of Death.
They'll play deserter, turn with the traitor breath,
Break the high bond we made, and sell Love's trust
And sacramental covenant to the dust.
– Oh, never a doubt but, somewhere, I shall wake,
And give what's left of love again, and make
New friends, now strangers . . . .

But the best I've known
Stays here, and changes, breaks, grows old, is blown
About the winds of the world, and fades from brains
Of living men, and dies.

Nothing remains.
O dear my loves, O faithless, once again
This one last gift I give: that after men
Shall know, and later lovers, far-removed,
Praise you, 'All these were lovely'; say, 'He loved.'

Rupert Brooke

The Soldier

IF I should die, think only this of me:
That there's some corner of a foreign field
That is for ever England. There shall be
In that rich earth a richer dust concealed;
A dust whom England bore, shaped, made aware,
Gave once her flowers to love, her ways to roam;
A body of England's, breathing English air,
Washed by the rivers, blest by suns of home.
And think, this heart, all evil shed away,
A pulse in the eternal mind, no less
Gives somewhere back the thoughts by England given;
Her sights and sounds; dreams happy as her day;
And laughter, learnt of friends; and gentleness,
In hearts at peace, under an English heaven.

Rupert Brooke

From Dewy Dreams

FROM dewy dreams, my soul, arise,
From love's deep slumber and from death,
For lo! the trees are full of sighs
Whose leaves the morn admonisheth.

Eastward the gradual dawn prevails
Where softly-burning fires appear,
Making to tremble all those veils
Of grey and golden gossamer.

While sweetly, gently, secretly,
The flowery bells of morn are stirred
And the wise choirs of faery
Begin (innumerous!) to be heard.

James Joyce

At That Hour

A T that hour when all things have repose,
O lonely watcher of the skies,
Do you hear the night wind and the sighs
Of harps playing unto Love to unclose
The pale gates of sunrise?

When all things repose, do you alone
Awake to hear the sweet harps play
To Love before him on his way,
And the night wind answering in antiphon
Till night is overgone?

Play on, invisible harps, unto Love,
Whose way in heaven is aglow
At that hour when soft lights come and go,
Soft sweet music in the air above
And in the earth below.

James Joyce

In the Dark Pine-Wood

IN the dark pine-wood
I would we lay,
In deep cool shadow
At noon of day.

How sweet to lie there,
Sweet to kiss,
Where the great pine-forest
Enaisled is!

Thy kiss descending
Sweeter were
With a soft tumult
Of thy hair.

O unto the pine-wood
At noon of day
Come with me now,
Sweet love, away.

James Joyce

Happiness

EVER again to breathe pure happiness,
So happy that we gave away our toy?
We smiled at nothings, needing no caress?
Have we not laughed too often since with Joy?
Have we not stolen too strange and sorrowful wrongs
For her hands' pardoning? The sun may cleanse,
And time, and starlight. Life will sing great songs,
And gods will show us pleasures more than men's.

Yet heaven looks smaller than the old doll's-home,
No nestling place is left in bluebell bloom,
And the wide arms of trees have lost their scope.
The former happiness is unreturning:
Boys' griefs are not so grievous as our yearning,
Boys have no sadness sadder than our hope.

Wilfred Owen

ONLY a man harrowing clods
   In a slow silent walk
With an old horse that stumbles and nods
  Half asleep as they stalk.

Only thin smoke without flame
From the heaps of couch-grass;
Yet this will go onward the same
Though Dynasties pass.

Yonder a maid and her wight
Come whispering by:
War's annals will fade into night
Ere their story die.

Thomas Hardy

Hédauville

THE sunshine on the long white road
That ribboned down the hill,
The velvet clematis that clung
Around your window-sill
Are waiting for you still.

Again the shadowed pool shall break
In dimples at your feet,
And when the thrush sings in your wood,
Unknowing you may meet
Another stranger, Sweet.

And if he is not quite so old
As the boy you used to know,
And less proud, too, and worthier,
You may not let him go –
(And daisies are truer than passion-flowers)

It will be better so.

Roland Leighton

Autumn

NOW leafy winds are blowing cold,
And South by West the sun goes down,
A quiet huddles up the fold
In sheltered corners of the brown.

Like scattered fire the wild fruit strews
The ground beneath the blowing tree,
And there the busy squirrel hews
His deep and secret granary.

And when the night comes starry clear,
The lonely quail complains beside
The glistening waters on the mere
Where widowed Beauties yet abide.

And I, too, make my own complaint
Upon a reed I plucked in June,
And love to hear it echoed faint
Upon another heart in tune.

Francis Ledwidge

If I Had a Broomstick

IF I had a broomstick, and knew how to ride it,
I'd fly through the windows when Jane goes to tea,
And over the tops of the chimneys I'd guide it,
To lands where no children are cripples like me;
I'd run on the rocks with the crabs and the sea,
Where soft red anemones close when you touch;
If I had a broomstick, and knew how to ride it,
If I had a broomstick instead of a crutch!

Patrick R. Chalmers

The Fool

SINCE the wise men have not spoken, I speak that am
only a fool;
A fool that hath loved his folly,
Yea, more than the wise men their books or their counting
houses or their quiet homes,
Or their fame in men's mouths;
A fool that in all his days hath done never a prudent thing,
Never hath counted the cost, nor recked if another reaped
The fruit of his mighty sowing, content to scatter the seed;
A fool that is unrepentant, and that soon at the end of all
Shall laugh in his lonely heart as the ripe ears fall to the
reaping-hooks
And the poor are filled that were empty,
Tho' he go hungry.
I have squandered the splendid years that the Lord God
gave to my youth
In attempting impossible things, deeming them alone
worth the toil.

Was it folly or grace? Not men shall judge me, but God.

I have squandered the splendid years:

Lord, if I had the years I would squander them over again,

Aye, fling them from me!

For this I have heard in my heart, that a man shall scatter, not hoard,

Shall do the deed of to-day, nor take thought of tomorrow's teen,

Shall not bargain or huxter with God; or was it a jest of Christ's

And is this my sin before men, to have taken Him at His word?

The lawyers have sat in council, the men with the keen, long faces,

And said, 'This man is a fool,' and others have said, 'He blasphemeth';

And the wise have pitied the fool that hath striven to give a life

In the world of time and space among the bulks of actual
   things,
To a dream that was dreamed in the heart, and that only
   the heart could hold.
O wise men, riddle me this: what if the dream come true?
What if the dream come true? and if millions unborn shall
   dwell
In the house that I shaped in my heart, the noble house of
   my thought?
Lord, I have staked my soul, I have staked the lives of my
   kin
On the truth of Thy dreadful word. Do not remember my
   failures,
But remember this my faith
And so I speak.
Yea, ere my hot youth pass, I speak to my people and say:
Ye shall be foolish as I; ye shall scatter, not save;

Ye shall venture your all, lest ye lose what is more than all;
Ye shall call for a miracle, taking Christ at His word.
And for this I will answer, O people, answer here and
    hereafter,
O people that I have loved, shall we not answer together?

Pádraig Pearse

A Cradle Song

THE angels are stooping
Above your bed;
They weary of trooping
With the whimpering dead.

God's laughing in Heaven
To see you so good;
The Sailing Seven
Are gay with His mood.

I sigh that kiss you,
For I must own
That I shall miss you
When you have grown.

William Butler Yeats

Brown Penny

I WHISPERED, 'I am too young,'
And then, 'I am old enough';
Wherefore I threw a penny
To find out if I might love.
'Go and love, go and love, young man,
If the lady be young and fair.'
Ah, penny, brown penny, brown penny,
I am looped in the loops of her hair.

O love is the crooked thing,
There is nobody wise enough
To find out all that is in it,
For he would be thinking of love
Till the stars had run away
And the shadows eaten the moon.
Ah, penny, brown penny, brown penny,
One cannot begin it too soon.

William Butler Yeats

A Dream

I HEARD the dogs howl in the moonlight night;
I went to the window to see the sight;
All the Dead that ever I knew
Going one by one and two by two.

On they pass'd, and on they pass'd;
Townsfellows all, from first to last;
Born in the moonlight of the lane,
Quench'd in the heavy shadow again.

Schoolmates, marching as when they play'd
At soldiers once – but now more staid;
Those were the strangest sight to me
Who were drown'd, I knew, in the awful sea.

Straight and handsome folk, bent and weak, too;
Some that I loved, and gasp'd to speak to;
Some but a day in their churchyard bed;
Some that I had not known were dead.

A long, long crowd – where each seem'd lonely,
Yet of them all there was one, one only,
Raised a head or look'd my way;
She linger'd a moment – she might not stay.

How long since I saw that fair pale face!
Ah! Mother dear! might I only place
My head on thy breast, a moment to rest,
While thy hand on my tearful cheek were prest!

On, on, a moving bridge they made
Across the moon-stream, from shade to shade,
Young and old, women and men;
Many long-forgot, but remembered then,

And first there came a bitter laughter;
A sound of tears a moment after;
And then a music so lofty and gay,
That every morning, day by day,
I strive to recall it if I may.

William Allingham

Star-Talk

'ARE you awake, Gemelli,
  This frosty night?'
'We'll be awake till reveillé,
Which is Sunrise,' say the Gemelli,
'It's no good trying to go to sleep:
If there's wine to be got we'll drink it deep,
But rest is hopeless to-night,
But rest is hopeless to-night.'

'Are you cold too, poor Pleiads,
This frosty night?'
'Yes, and so are the Hyads:
See us cuddle and hug,' say the Pleiads,
'All six in a ring: it keeps us warm:
We huddle together like birds in a storm:
It's bitter weather to-night,
It's bitter weather to-night.'

'What do you hunt, Orion,
This starry night?'
'The Ram, the Bull and the Lion,
And the Great Bear,' says Orion,
'With my starry quiver and beautiful belt
I am trying to find a good thick pelt
To warm my shoulders to-night,
To warm my shoulders to-night.'

'Did you hear that, Great She-bear,
This frosty night?
'Yes, he's talking of stripping me bare
Of my own big fur,' says the She-bear,
'I'm afraid of the man and his terrible arrow:
The thought of it chills my bones to the marrow,
And the frost so cruel to-night!
And the frost so cruel to-night!'

'How is your trade, Aquarius,
This frosty night?'
'Complaints is many and various
And my feet are cold,' says Aquarius,
'There's Venus objects to Dolphin-scales,
And Mars to Crab-spawn found in my pails,
And the pump has frozen to-night,
And the pump has frozen to-night.'

Robert Graves

The Kingfisher

IT was the Rainbow gave thee birth,
And left thee all her lovely hues;
And, as her mother's name was Tears,
So runs it in my blood to choose
For haunts the lonely pools, and keep
In company with trees that weep.
Go you and, with such glorious hues,
Live with proud peacocks in green parks;
On lawns as smooth as shining glass,
Let every feather show its marks;
Get thee on boughs and clap thy wings
Before the windows of proud kings.
Nay, lovely Bird, thou art not vain;
Thou hast no proud, ambitious mind;
I also love a quiet place
That's green, away from all mankind;
A lonely pool, and let a tree
Sigh with her bosom over me.

William Henry Davies

The Early Morning

The moon on the one hand, the dawn on the
    other:
The moon is my sister, the dawn is my
      brother.
The moon on my left and the dawn on my
      right.
My brother, good morning: my sister, good
      night.

Hilaire Belloc

Sheep

WHEN I was once in Baltimore
      A man came up to me and cried,
'Come, I have eighteen hundred sheep,
And we will sail on Tuesday's tide.

'If you will sail with me, young man,
I'll pay you fifty shillings down;
These eighteen hundred sheep I take
From Baltimore to Glasgow town.'

He paid me fifty shillings down,
I sailed with eighteen hundred sheep;
We soon had cleared the harbour's mouth,
We soon were in the salt sea deep.

The first night we were out at sea
Those sheep were quiet in their mind;
The second night they cried with fear
They smelt no pastures in the wind.

They sniffed, poor things, for their green fields,
They cried so loud I could not sleep:
For fifty thousand shillings down
I would not sail again with sheep.

William Henry Davies

Home Thoughts in Laventie

GREEN gardens in Laventie!
Soldiers only know the street
Where the mud is churned and splashed about
By battle-wending feet;
And yet beside one stricken house there is a glimpse of grass.
Look for it when you pass.

Beyond the church whose pitted spire
Seems balanced on a strand
Of swaying stone and tottering brick
Two roofless ruins stand,
And here behind the wreckage where the back wall
   should have been
We found a garden green.

The grass was never trodden on,
The little path of gravel
Was overgrown with celandine,
No other folk did travel
Along its weedy surface, but the nimble-footed mouse
Running from house to house.

So all among the vivid blades
Of soft and tender grass
We lay, nor heard the limber wheels
That pass and ever pass,
In noisy continuity until their stony rattle
Seems in itself a battle.

At length we rose up from this ease
Of tranquil happy mind,
And searched the garden's little length
Some new pleasaunce to find;
And there, some yellow daffodils and jasmine hanging high
Did rest the tired eye.

The fairest and most fragrant
Of the many sweets we found,
Was a little bush of Daphne flower
Upon a grassy mound,
And so thick were the blossoms set and so divine the scent
That we were well content.

Hungry for spring, I bent my head,
The perfume fanned my face,
And all my soul was dancing
In that little lovely place,
Dancing with a measured step from wrecked and shattered
    towns
Away... upon the Downs.

I saw green banks of daffodil,
Slim poplars in the breeze,
Great tan-brown hares in gusty March
A-courting on the leas;
And meadows with their glittering streams, and silver
    scurrying dace,
Home – what a perfect place!

Edward Wyndham Tennant

Le Jardin

THE lily's withered chalice falls
　　Around its rod of dusty gold,
And from the beech-trees on the wold
The last wood-pigeon coos and calls.

The gaudy leonine sunflower
Hangs black and barren on its stalk,
And down the windy garden walk
The dead leaves scatter, – hour by hour.

Pale privet – petals white as milk
Are blown into a snowy mass:
The roses lie upon the grass
Like little shreds of crimson silk.

Oscar Wilde

Into Battle

THE naked earth is warm with Spring,
    And with green grass and bursting trees
Leans to the sun's gaze glorying,
    And quivers in the sunny breeze;
And life is Colour and Warmth and Light,
    And a striving evermore for these;
And he is dead who will not fight,
    And who dies fighting has increase.
The fighting man shall from the sun
    Take warmth, and life from glowing earth;
Speed with the light-foot winds to run
    And with the trees to newer birth;
And find, when fighting shall be done,
    Great rest, and fullness after dearth.
All the bright company of Heaven
    Hold him in their bright comradeship –
The Dog star, and the Sisters Seven,
    Orion's belt and sworded hip:
The woodland trees that stand together,

They stand to him each one a friend;
They gently speak in the windy weather;
They guide to valley and ridge's end.
The kestrel hovering by day,
And the little owls that call by night,
Bid him be swift and keen as they,
As keen of ear, as swift of sight.
The blackbird sings to him: 'Brother, brother,
If this be the last song you shall sing,
Sing well, for you may not sing another;
Brother, sing.'
In dreary doubtful waiting hours,
Before the brazen frenzy starts,
The horses show him nobler powers;
O patient eyes, courageous hearts!
And when the burning moment breaks,
And all things else are out of mind,
And only joy of battle takes
Him by the throat and makes him blind,

Through joy and blindness he shall know,
Not caring much to know, that still
Nor lead nor steel shall reach him, so
That it be not the Destined Will.
The thundering line of battle stands,
And in the air Death moans and sings;
But Day shall clasp him with strong hands,
And Night shall fold him in soft wings.

Julian Grenfell

Overheard on a Saltmarsh

NYMPH, nymph, what are your beads?
Green glass, goblin. Why do you stare at them?
Give them me.
          No.

Give them me. Give them me.
          No.

Then I will howl all night in the reeds,
Lie in the mud and howl for them.

Goblin, why do you love them so?

They are better than stars or water,
Better than voices of winds that sing,
Better than any man's fair daughter,
Your green glass beads on a silver ring.

Hush, I stole them out of the moon.

Give me your beads, I desire them.
                No.

I will howl in the deep lagoon
For your green glass beads, I love them so.
Give them me. Give them.
                No.

Harold Monro

A Flower is Looking through the Ground

A FLOWER is looking through the ground,
Blinking at the April weather;
Now a child has seen the flower:
Now they go and play together.

Now it seems the flower will speak,
And will call the child its brother –
But, oh strange forgetfulness! –
They don't recognize each other.

Harold Monro

Endymion

THE apple trees are hung with gold,
  And birds are loud in Arcady,
The sheep lie bleating in the fold,
The wild goat runs across the wold,
But yesterday his love he told,
I know he will come back to me.
O rising moon! O Lady moon!
Be you my lover's sentinel,
You cannot choose but know him well,
For he is shod with purple shoon,
You cannot choose but know my love,
For he a shepherd's crook doth bear,
And he is soft as any dove,
And brown and curly is his hair.

The turtle now has ceased to call
Upon her crimson-footed groom,
The grey wolf prowls about the stall,
The lily's singing seneschal

Sleeps in the lily-bell, and all
The violet hills are lost in gloom.
O risen moon! O holy moon!
Stand on the top of Helice,
And if my own true love you see,
Ah! if you see the purple shoon,
The hazel crook, the lad's brown hair,
The goat-skin wrapped about his arm,
Tell him that I am waiting where
The rushlight glimmers in the Farm.

The falling dew is cold and chill,
And no bird sings in Arcady,
The little fauns have left the hill,
Even the tired daffodil
Has closed its gilded doors, and still
My lover comes not back to me.
False moon! False moon! O waning moon!
Where is my own true lover gone,
Where are the lips vermilion,

The shepherd's crook, the purple shoon?
Why spread that silver pavilion,
Why wear that veil of drifting mist?
Ah! thou hast young Endymion,
Thou hast the lips that should be kissed!

Oscar Wilde

The Cherry Trees

THE cherry trees bend over and are shedding,
    On the old road where all that passed are dead,
Their petals, strewing the grass as for a wedding
This early May morn when there is none to wed.

Edward Thomas

A Thing of Beauty (Endymion)

A THING of beauty is a joy for ever:
Its loveliness increases; it will never
Pass into nothingness; but still will keep
A bower quiet for us, and a sleep
Full of sweet dreams, and health, and quiet breathing.
Therefore, on every morrow, are we wreathing
A flowery band to bind us to the earth,
Spite of despondence, of the inhuman dearth
Of noble natures, of the gloomy days,
Of all the unhealthy and o'er-darkn'd ways
Made for our searching: yes, in spite of all,
Some shape of beauty moves away the pall
From our dark spirits. Such the sun, the moon,
Trees old and young, sprouting a shady boon
For simple sheep; and such are daffodils
With the green world they live in; and clear rills
That for themselves a cooling covert make
'Gainst the hot season; the mid-forest brake,
Rich with a sprinkling of fair musk-rose blooms:

And such too is the grandeur of the dooms
We have imagined for the mighty dead;
An endless fountain of immortal drink,
Pouring unto us from the heaven's brink.

John Keats

The Wild Swans At Coole

THE trees are in their autumn beauty,
The woodland paths are dry,
Under the October twilight the water
Mirrors a still sky;
Upon the brimming water among the stones
Are nine-and-fifty swans.

The nineteenth autumn has come upon me
Since I first made my count;
I saw, before I had well finished,
All suddenly mount
And scatter wheeling in great broken rings
Upon their clamorous wings.

I have looked upon those brilliant creatures,
And now my heart is sore.
All's changed since I, hearing at twilight,
The first time on this shore,
The bell-beat of their wings above my head,
Trod with a lighter tread.

Unwearied still, lover by lover,
They paddle in the cold
Companionable streams or climb the air;
Their hearts have not grown old;
Passion or conquest, wander where they will,
Attend upon them still.

But now they drift on the still water,
Mysterious, beautiful;
Among what rushes will they build,
By what lake's edge or pool
Delight men's eyes when I awake some day
To find they have flown away?

William Butler Yeats

Thoughts at the Trysting Stile

COME, May, and hang a white flag on each thorn,
Make truce with earth and heaven; the April child
Now hides her sulky face deep in the morn
Of your new flowers by the water wild
And in the ripples of the rising grass,
And rushes bent to let the south wind pass
On with her tumult of swift nomad wings,
And broken domes of downy dandelion.
Only in spasms now the blackbird sings.
The hour is all a-dream.

Nets of woodbine
Throw woven shadows over dreaming flowers,
And dreaming, a bee-luring lily bends
Its tender bell where blue dyke-water cowers
Thro' briars and folded ferns, and gripping ends
Of wild convolvulus.

The lark's sky-way
Is desolate.
I watch an apple-spray
Beckon across a wall as if it knew
I wait the calling of the orchard maid.
Only I feel she will come in blue,
With yellow on her hair, and two curls strayed
Out of her comb's loose stocks, and I shall steal
Behind and lay my hands upon her eyes,
'Look not, but be my Psyche!'

And her peal
Of laughter will ring far, and as she tries
For freedom I will call her names of flowers
That climb up walls; then thro' the twilight hours
We'll talk about the loves of ancient queens,
And kisses like wasp-honey, false and sweet,
And how we are entangled in love's snares
Like wind-looped flowers.

Francis Ledwidge

To the Coming Spring

O PUNCTUAL Spring!
   We had forgotten in this winter town
The days of Summer and the long, long eves.
But now you come on airy wing,
With busy fingers spilling baby-leaves
On all the bushes, and a faint green down
On ancient trees, and everywhere
Your warm breath soft with kisses
Stirs the wintry air,
And waking us to unimagined blisses.
Your lightest footprints in the grass
Are marked by painted crocus-flowers
And heavy-headed daffodils,
While little trees blush faintly as you pass.
The morning and the night
You bathe with heavenly showers,
And scatter scentless violets on the rounded hills,
Drop beneath leafless woods pale primrose posies.
With magic key, in the new evening light,

You are unlocking buds that keep the roses;
The purple lilac soon will blow above the wall
And bended boughs in orchards whitely bloom –
We had forgotten in the Winter's gloom . . .
Soon we shall hear the cuckoo call!

Margaret Mackenzie

Alms in Autumn

SPINDLE-WOOD, spindle-wood, will you
lend me, pray,
A little flaming lantern to guide me on
　　my way?
The fairies all have vanished from the meadow and the
　　glen,
And I would fain go seeking till I find them once again.
Lend me now a lantern that I may bear a light
To find the hidden pathway in the darkness of the night.

Ash-tree, ash-tree, throw me, if you please,
Throw me down a slender branch of russet-gold keys.
I fear the gates of Fairyland may all be shut so fast
That nothing but your magic keys will ever take me past.
I'll tie them to my girdle, and as I go along
My heart will find a comfort in the tinkle of their song.

Holly-bush, holly-bush, help me in my task,
A pocketful of berries is all the alms I ask:
A pocketful of berries to thread in golden strands
(I would not go a-visiting with nothing in my hands).
So fine will be the rosy chains, so gay, so glossy bright,
They'll set the realms of Fairyland all dancing with delight.

Rose Fyleman

Sonnet on Hearing the Dies Irae Sung in the Sistine Chapel

NAY, Lord, not thus! white lilies in the spring,
Sad olive-groves, or silver-breasted dove,
Teach me more clearly of Thy life and love
Than terrors of red flame and thundering.
The hillside vines dear memories of Thee bring:
A bird at evening flying to its nest
Tells me of One who had no place of rest:
I think it is of Thee the sparrows sing.
Come rather on some autumn afternoon,
When red and brown are burnished on the leaves,
And the fields echo to the gleaner's song,
Come when the splendid fullness of the moon
Looks down upon the rows of golden sheaves,
And reap Thy harvest: we have waited long.

Oscar Wilde

He Wishes for the Cloths of Heaven

HAD I the heavens' embroidered cloths,
Enwrought with golden and silver light,
The blue and the dim and the dark cloths
Of night and light and the half-light,
I would spread the cloths under your feet:
But I, being poor, have only my dreams;
I have spread my dreams under your feet;
Tread softly because you tread on my dreams.

William Butler Yeats

Very Nearly!

I NEVER *quite* saw fairy-folk
A-dancing in the glade,
Where, just beyond the hollow oak,
Their broad green rings are laid:
But, while behind that oak I hid,
One day I very nearly did!

I never quite saw mermaids rise
Above the twilight sea,
When sands, left wet, 'neath sunset skies,
Are blushing rosily:
But all alone, those rocks amid –
One night I very nearly did!

I never quite saw Goblin Grim
Who haunts our lumber room
And pops his head above the rim
Of that oak chest's deep gloom:
But once when Mother raised the lid –
I very, very nearly did!

Queenie Scott-Hopper

What the Thrush Says

'COME and see! Come and see!'
The Thrush pipes out of the hawthorn-tree:

And I and Dicky on tiptoe go
To see what treasures he wants to show.
His call is clear as a call can be
And 'Come and see!' he says:
'Come and see!'

'Come and see! Come and see!'
His house is there in the hawthorn-tree:
The neatest house that ever you saw,
Built all of mosses and twigs and straw:
The folk who built were his wife and he
And 'Come and see!' he says:
'Come and see!'

'Come and see! Come and see!'
Within this house there are treasures three:

So warm and snug in its curve they lie
Like three bright bits out of Spring's blue sky.
We would not hurt them, he knows; not we!
So 'Come and see!' he says:
'Come and see!'

'Come and see! Come and see!'
No thrush was ever so proud as he!
His bright-eyed lady has left those eggs
For just five minutes to stretch her legs.
He's keeping guard in the hawthorn-tree,
And 'Come and see!' he says:
'Come and see!'

'Come and see! Come and see!'
He has no fear of the boys and me.
He came and shared in our meals, you know,
In hungry times of the frost and snow.
So now we share in his Secret Tree
Where 'Come and see!' he says:
'Come and see!'

Queenie Scott-Hopper

The Sunset Garden

I CAN see from the window a little brown house,
And the garden goes up to the top of the hill.
    And the sun comes each day,
    And slips down away
At the end of the garden an' sleeps there . . . until
The daylight comes climbing up over the hill.

I do wish I lived in the little brown house,
Then at night I'd go out to the garden, an' creep
    Up . . . up . . . then I'd stop,
    An' lean over the top,
At the end of the garden, an' so I could peep,
And see what the sun looks like when it's asleep.

Marion St John Webb

To Betsey-Jane, on her Desiring to go Incontinently to Heaven

My Betsey-Jane, it would not do,
For what would Heaven make of you,
A little, honey-loving bear,
Among the Blessed Babies there?

Nor do you dwell with us in vain
Who tumble and get up again
And try, with bruised knees, to smile –
Sweet, you are blessed all the while

And we in you: so wait, they'll come
To take your hand and fetch you home,
In Heavenly leaves to play at tents
With all the Holy Innocents.

Helen Parry Eden

Behind the Closed Eye

I walk the old frequented ways
That wind around the tangled braes,
I live again the sunny days
Ere I the city knew.

And scenes of old again are born,
The woodbine lassoing the thorn,
And drooping Ruth-like in the corn
The poppies weep the dew.

Above me in their hundred schools
The magpies bend their young to rules,
And like an apron full of jewels
The dewy cobweb swings.

And frisking in the stream below
The troutlets make the circles flow,
And the hungry crane doth watch them grow
As a smoker does his rings.

Above me smokes the little town,
With its whitewashed walls and roofs of brown
And its octagon spire toned smoothly down
As the holy minds within.

And wondrous impudently sweet,
Half of him passion, half conceit,
The blackbird calls adown the street
Like the piper of Hamelin.

I hear him, and I feel the lure
Drawing me back to the homely moor,
I'll go and close the mountain's door
On the city's strife and din.

Francis Ledwidge

All is Spirit and Part of Me

A GREATER lover none can be,
And All is Spirit and Part of Me.
I am sway of the rolling hills,
And breath from the great wide plains;
I am born of a thousand storms,
And grey with the rushing rains;
I have stood with the age-long rocks,
And flowered with the meadow sweet;
I have fought with the wind-worn firs
And bent with the ripening wheat;
I have watched with the solemn clouds,
And dreamt with the moorland pools;
I have raced with the water's whirl,
And lain where their anger cools;
I have hovered as strong-winged bird,
And swooped as I saw my prey;
I have risen with cold grey dawn,
and flamed in the dying day;
For all is Spirit and Part of Me,
And greater lover none can be.

Lettice D'Oyly Walters

The Wayfarer

THE beauty of the world hath made me sad,
This beauty that will pass;
Sometimes my heart hath shaken with great joy
To see a leaping squirrel in a tree,
Or a red lady-bird upon a stalk,
Or little rabbits in a field at evening,
Lit by a slanting sun,
Or some green hill, where shadows drifted by,
Some quiet hill, where mountainy man hath sown
And soon would reap; near to the gate of Heaven;
Or children with bare feet upon the sands
Of some ebbed sea, or playing on the streets
Of little towns in Connacht,
Things young and happy.
And then my heart hath told me:
These will pass,
Will pass and change, will die and be no more,
Things bright and green, things young and happy;
And I have gone upon my way
Sorrowful.

Pádraig Pearse

No Song

I LOOSE the secrets of my soul
And mint my heart to heavy words
Lest you should need to ask a dole
Of singing from the winds and birds –
You will not heed nor bear my soul.

I coin again a greater sum
Of silence, and you will not heed:
The fallow spaces call you 'Come,
The season's ripe to sow the seed' –
Both I and these are better dumb.

I have no way to make you hear,
No song will echo in your heart;
Now must I with the fading year
Fade. Without meeting we must part –
No song nor silence you will hear.

Joseph Mary Plunkett

The Fairies

Up the airy mountain,
  Down the rushy glen,
We daren't go a-hunting
For fear of little men;
Wee folk, good folk,
Trooping all together;
Green jacket, red cap,
And white owl's feather!

Down along the rocky shore
Some make their home,
They live on crispy pancakes
Of yellow tide-foam;
Some in the reeds
Of the black mountain lake,
With frogs for their watch-dogs,
All night awake.
High on the hill-top
The old King sits;

He is now so old and gray
He's nigh lost his wits.
With a bridge of white mist
Columbkill he crosses,
On his stately journeys
From Slieveleague to Rosses;
Or going up with music
On cold starry nights
To sup with the Queen
Of the gay Northern Lights.

They stole little Bridget
For seven years long;
When she came down again
Her friends were all gone.
They took her lightly back,
Between the night and morrow,
They thought that she was fast asleep,
But she was dead with sorrow.

They have kept her ever since
Deep within the lake,
On a bed of flag-leaves,
Watching till she wake.
By the craggy hill-side,
Through the mosses bare,
They have planted thorn-trees
For pleasure here and there.
If any man so daring
As dig them up in spite,
He shall find their sharpest thorns
In his bed at night.

Up the airy mountain,
Down the rushy glen,
We daren't go a-hunting
For fear of little men;
Wee folk, good folk,
Trooping all together;
Green jacket, red cap,
And white owl's feather!

William Allingham

Black and White

I MET a man along the road
      To Withernsea;
Was ever anything so dark, so pale
            As he?
His hat, his clothes, his tie, his boots
            Were black as black
                  Could be,
And midst of all was a cold white face,
And eyes that looked wearily.

The road was bleak and straight and flat
            To Withernsea,
Gaunt poles with shrilling wires their weird
            Did dree;
On the sky stood out, on the swollen sky
            The black blood veins
                  Of tree
After tree, as they beat from the face
Of the wind which they could not flee.

And in the fields along the road
  To Withernsea,
Swart crows sat huddled on the ground
  Disconsolately,
While overhead the seamews wheeled, and
      skirled
    In glee;
But the black cows stood, and cropped where
      they stood,
  And never heeded thee,
O dark pale man, with the weary eyes,
  On the road to Withernsea.

H. H. Abbott

The Oxen

CHRISTMAS Eve, and twelve of the clock.
'Now they are all on their knees,'
An elder said as we sat in a flock
By the embers in hearthside ease.

We pictured the meek mild creatures where
They dwelt in their strawy pen,
Nor did it occur to one of us there
To doubt they were kneeling then.

So fair a fancy few would weave
In these years! Yet, I feel,
If someone said on Christmas Eve,
'Come; see the oxen kneel

'In the lonely barton by yonder coomb
Our childhood used to know,'
I should go with him in the gloom,
Hoping it might be so.

Thomas Hardy

Pippa's Song

THE year's at the spring,
  And day's at the morn;
Morning's at seven;
The hill-side's dew-pearl'd;
The lark's on the wing;
The snail's on the thorn;
God's in His heaven –
All's right with the world!

Robert Browning

BIOGRAPHIES

Abbott, H. H. *c.C19th–c. early C20th*
Author of a poetry book entitled *Black and White* and also *An Essex Harvest and Other Poems.*

Allingham, William *1824–1889*
Born in Ballyshannon, Co. Donegal, son of a bank manager of English descent, he worked as a customs official until 1870, after which he devoted himself exclusively to poetry and writing.

Belloc, Hilaire 1870–1953
Anglo-French writer and historian, orator, satirist and political activist. A devout Catholic, he frequently collaborated in his writing work with G. K. Chesterton.

Brady, Edwin James *1869–1952*
Irish-Australian journalist, writer and publisher with a lifelong interest in sailing and the sea. His first poem was published in 1891 and he continued to write and publish prolifically.

Brooke, Rupert *1887–1915*
An established poet when he enlisted in 1914, he saw action at Antwerp. While he was en route to fight in the Dardanelles he contracted blood poisoning and died.

Browning, Robert *1812–1889*
Prominent Victorian poet who spent much of his life in Italy with his wife, the poet Elizabeth Barrett. He was revered in Britain during his lifetime and is buried in Westminster Abbey.

Chalmers, Patrick R. *1872–1942*
Born in Ireland, he worked as a banker in London. He wrote prolifically on many topics for popular journals of the day. His first book, *Green Days and Blue Days* was published when he was 40.

Chesterton, G. K. *1874–1936*
A renowned man of letters and famous wit, convert to and apologist for Catholicism, Chesterton wrote 80 books, hundreds of poems and short stories and thousands of essays on a wide range of subjects.

Davies, W. H. *1871–1940*
Born in Monmouthshire, Wales, Davies worked variously as a labourer and travelling pedlar. His work concentrates on nature and life on the road, and his most famous and quoted poem is 'Leisure'.

de la Mare, Walter *1873–1958*
Related on his mother's side to Robert Browning, de la Mare started writing poetry for adults and children in 1895. He is famous for the dreamlike, slightly ghostly quality of much of his work.

D'Oyly Walters, Lettice *1880s–(?)*
A poet and compiler of several anthologies, including *An Anthology of Recent Poetry* and *The Year's At The Spring*. Both books were published by Harrap and included the same poems, though the latter was a larger format and was illustrated by Harry

Clarke. Also compiled *Irish Poets of Today* in 1921.

Eden, Helen Parry *1872(?)–1895*
Born in London, she was educated at Roedean, Manchester University and King's College Art School. Her poetry was published in *Punch, Pall Mall* magazine and *The Catholic Messenger.*

Fyleman, Rose *1877–1957*
A trained singer who taught singing in her sister's school, she was also a writer and poet. She wrote many poems about fairies and was one of the most successful children's writers of her generation.

Graves, Robert *1895–1985*
A poet, lecturer and novelist who fought courageously in the First World War and drew on his experiences for much of his writing. He also wrote widely on classical themes.

Grenfell, Julian *1888–1915*
Awarded the DSO for bravery in the Great War, he was fatally wounded near Ypres in 1915. 'Into Battle' was one of the most popular poems of that war.

Hardy, Thomas *1840–1928*
A novelist and poet, Hardy was passionate about literature and rural life. He was awarded the Order of Merit in 1910 and in his lifetime was as famous as Dickens. His ashes are buried in Westminster Abbey.

Higgins, F. R. *1896–1941*
Born in Foxford, Co. Mayo, Higgins was a poet and theatre director. 'Father and Son' is his most famous poem and his best known work is a collection of poetry entitled *The Gap of Brightness.*

Joyce, James *1882–1941*
A giant of the Irish and world literary scenes, Joyce's novels are all set in his native Dublin. His most famous novel is *Ulysses,* and his popular *Pomes Penyeach,* priced at a shilling, contains 13 poems (a baker's dozen).

Keats, John *1795–1821*
One of England's most popular poets, Keats died young, before his reputation was established. Today, however, his prolific poetry is the most analysed in English literature.

Ledwidge, Francis *1887–1917*
Born in Slane, Co. Meath, he enlisted in the British army in 1914 and was killed in action at the Battle of Passchendaele. He is known as the 'poet of the blackbirds'.

Leighton, Roland *1858–1914*
An amateur poet killed in action in the First World War, he is more famous as the fiancé of the writer and pacifist Vera Brittain. His wartime grave is often covered in violets as a tribute to a poem he wrote for her.

141

MacDonagh, Thomas *1878–1916*
An Irish poet and nationalist and friend of Pádraig Pearse, he was a signatory to the Proclamation of the Republic. He was executed on 3 May 1916 for his part in the Easter Rising.

Mackenzie, Margaret *(?)–1955*
A playwright and novelist who was one of the founding members of the Catholic Poetry Society and a tireless member of the Catholic Women's League.

Masefield, John *1878–1967*
Masefield was born in Ledbury, Herefordshire, and trained as a sailor. A poet of huge reputation, he was made Poet Laureate in 1930, and held that office until his death. His ashes are buried in Westminster Abbey.

Meynell, Alice *1847–1922*
London-born Meynell published her first poetry collection in 1875 and was a regular contributor to Catholic and secular periodicals.

Monro, Harold *1879–1932*
Born in Brussels to Scottish parents, Monro was proprietor of the Poetry Bookshop in London. He published his first collection of poetry in 1906 and founded the *Poetry Review* to promote new writing.

Naidu, Sarojini *1879–1949*
A Cambridge-educated poet and politician, Naidu was known as the Nightingale of India. She was the first female president of the Indian National Congress. Her birthday is celebrated annually as World Women's Day.

Owen, Wilfred *1893–1918*
A decorated soldier who was killed just a few days before the Armistice, he is renowned as a technically accomplished poet, whose war poems are considered masters of their genre.

Pearse, Pádraig *1879–1916*
A teacher, barrister, writer, nationalist and political activist, he was one of the leaders of the Easter Rising of 1916. He was executed for his part in it on 3 May of that year.

Plunkett, Joseph Mary *1887–1916*
An Irish poet and nationalist, many of whose poems have a religious theme. He was one of the planners of the 1916 Rising and was executed on 4 May 1916 for his part in it.

Russell, George William *1867–1935*
Born in Lurgan, Co. Armagh, this Irish nationalist, theosophist, critic, poet, novelist and painter wrote under the pseudonym 'AE'. He was a lifelong friend of W. B. Yeats.

Scott-Hopper, Queenie *1881–1924*
Born in Co. Durham to a family of lawyers, very little is known about her life. Her poems and stories remained popular after her death and were taught in many schools.

Tennant, Edward Wyndham *1897–1916*
The son of Lord Glenconner, he started writing poetry when he was a child. He joined the Grenadier Guards and was sent to fight in France when war was declared. He died at the Battle of the Somme.

Thomas, Edward *1878–1917*
An Anglo-Welsh writer who is remembered as a war poet, although few of his poems have war as their subject. Killed at Arras in 1917, he is commemorated in Poet's Corner at Westminster Abbey.

Watson, William *1858–1935*
A prolific, Yorkshire-born poet, renowned for the political nature of his work. He was in line to be Poet Laureate after Tennyson's death, but his opposition to the Boer War led to his being passed over.

Webb, Marion St John *1888–1930*
The daughter of the poet Arthur St John Adcock, she was a prolific writer of novels and poems for children. Such is her popularity that many of her books are still in print.

Wilde, Oscar *1854–1900*
Famous for his wit and charm and renowned as a master of the epigram, he was imprisoned for offences against morality in 1895. His only published work after his release was 'The Ballad of Reading Gaol'.

Yeats, W. B. *1865–1939*
One of the foremost literary figures of the twentieth century, Yeats was the first Irishman to be awarded the Nobel Prize for literature. His poems draw heavily on nature, mysticism, myth and legend.

ACKNOWLEDGEMENTS

Every effort has been made to trace copyright holders not mentioned here. If there have been any omissions, the publisher would be happy to rectify this in a reprint.

For permission to reproduce copyright poems the publisher is indebted to the following:

The Early Morning by Hilaire Belloc reprinted by permission of Peters Fraser & Dunlop (www.petersfraserdunlop.com) on behalf of the Estate of Hilaire Belloc

Carcanet Press Ltd
Star-Talk by Robert Graves

The Society of Authors
Arabia, Full Moon, Nod and *The Song of the Mad Prince* by Walter de la Mare
Sea Fever and *Tewkesbury Road* by John Masefield